# Byblos: The History and Legacy of the Oldest Ancient Phoenician City

## By Charles River Editors

A picture of the Old City of Byblos

## About Charles River Editors

**Charles River Editors** is a boutique digital publishing company, specializing in bringing history back to life with educational and engaging books on a wide range of topics. Keep up to date with our new and free offerings with this 5 second sign up on our weekly mailing list, and visit Our Kindle Author Page to see other recently published Kindle titles.

We make these books for you and always want to know our readers' opinions, so we encourage you to leave reviews and look forward to publishing new and exciting titles each week.

# Introduction

**A picture of the Old City**

# Byblos

Of all the peoples of the ancient Near East, the Phoenicians are among the most recognizable but also perhaps the least understood. The Phoenicians never built an empire like the Egyptians and Assyrians; in fact, the Phoenicians never created a unified Phoenician state but instead existed as independent city-state kingdoms scattered throughout the Mediterranean region. However, despite the fact there was never a "Phoenician Empire," the Phoenicians proved to be more prolific in their exploration and colonization than any other peoples in world history until the Spanish during the Age of Discovery.

The Phoenicians were well-known across different civilizations throughout the ancient world, and their influence can be felt across much of the West today because they are credited with inventing the forerunner to the Greek alphabet, from which the Latin alphabet was directly derived. Nonetheless, the Phoenicians left behind few written texts, so modern historians have been forced to reconstruct their past through a variety of ancient Egyptians, Assyrian,

Babylonian, Greek, and Roman sources. It's not even clear what the Phoenicians called themselves, because the name "Phoenician" is derived from the Greek word "phoinix", which possibly relates to the dyes they produced and traded (Markoe 2000, 10). The mystery of the ancient Phoenicians is further compounded by the fact that archaeologists have only been able to excavate small sections of the three primary Phoenician cities: Byblos, Sidon, and Tyre.

Byblos, known today as Jubayl, has been known by many names over the ages: the Phoenicians called it Gebal; for the Egyptians it was Kepen or Kupna; the Assyrians and Akkadians referred to it as Gubla (this name was repeated throughout the Old Testament); the Arabs called it Jbeil, and eventually the European Crusaders gave it the name of Gibelet.[1] This lengthy etymology reflects the city's unique heritage significance, because Byblos is one of the oldest continuously inhabited cities ever to have existed in the world. The city was frequently mentioned in the great archives of antiquity, but its origins lie in the depths of prehistory. Its strategic location, with plenty of shipbuilding wood coming from the nearby mountains, made many powerful states eager to control the territory. Over time, Byblos and its surrounding area were occupied by the Amorites, Canaanites, Phoenicians, Assyrians, Persians, Macedonians, Romans, Arabs, Crusaders, Mamelukes, and Ottomans.

From the earliest of times, Byblos was an active commercial center, trading extensively with Egypt, where it exported cedar wood from the Phoenician homelands in exchange for papyrus. As a result, Egypt would have a significant influence on the art and culture of Byblos, and the city quickly assumed a position of supremacy in the Mediterranean, thanks in part to its early use of writing. Archaeological evidence uncovered at the city show the existence of a Phoenician alphabet being used from as early as 1200 BCE, and the remains of Phoenician cities along the coast of Lebanon bear witness to the important role they played as a meeting place between the east and west, making it a focal point for the fusion of cultures in the ancient world. The Phoenicians did not generally seek political advantages or territorial expansion in their homeland–their interest was primarily in international trade.

As one of the oldest cities in the world, Byblos is a fascinating place, with its successive layers of debris representing millennia of human occupation. From the earliest times this coastal strip played a key role in connecting Arabia, Anatolia, Mesopotamia, Egypt, and the Aegean. Because of this, the history of the city cannot be told in isolation of its neighbors. From the Bronze Age Byblos had a special connection with Egypt, which ceased only with the invasion of the mysterious Sea Peoples at the end of the 2$^{nd}$ millennium BCE. Although difficult to pin down as a unified people, the Phoenicians were unique in their remarkable maritime achievements. Totally oriented to the sea, their journeys brought them to the edge of the known world, and their brave sailors returned with wonderful treasures. Since Phoenicia was for so many centuries the connecting link between the western lands of Europe and Africa on the one hand, and the Near

---

[1] For the sake of clarity, this text will generally use Byblos to refer to the site, regardless of the period or people involved.

Eastern lands of Arabia and Mesopotamia on the other, as well as between Asia Minor and Palestine, it is not surprising that many divergent religions have and continue to exist in the region. Furthermore, the Lebanon Mountains, with their many valleys and difficulty of access, have served as the refuge for a great number and variety of persecuted religious sects, giving them the opportunity to survive as they disappeared elsewhere.

Much of the coastline of the area is heavily urbanized, which likely obscures many further interesting structures that might completely change the narrative of the site if they were uncovered. Moreover, many of the archaeological remains are openly exposed to the elements. The construction of a modern jetty has modified the coastal configuration, which has exacerbated the problem of wave energy from the strong storms that regularly batter the coast. Some attempts at coastal engineering have been made to prevent environmental change, and the site's environmental heritage significance has been recognized (being the first archaeological coastline in Lebanon to also become a protected natural landscape), but further steps will need to be taken preserve the unique heritage of Byblos.

Compared to its splendid past, modern Jubayl is a relatively small town dependent on tourism, as evidenced by the renovated souks and shops catering to visitors. The famous crusader castle has the distinction of being located within a vast field of archaeological ruins left behind by the greatest civilizations of antiquity, but many of the structures face constant threat by modern development and rebuilding projects, all of which threaten to destroy what's left of this city's unique heritage landscape.

*Byblos: The History and Legacy of the Oldest Ancient Phoenician City* chronicles the tumultuous history of one of the most important cities of antiquity. Along with pictures depicting important people, places, and events, you will learn about Byblos like never before.

Byblos: The History and Legacy of the Oldest Ancient Phoenician City
About Charles River Editors
Introduction
   One of the Oldest Cities in the World
   An Egyptian Vassal
   The Phoenicians
   Chapter 2: Early Phoenician History
   The Phoenician Entrepôt
   Clash of Civilizations
   Byblos in the Modern Period
   Online Resources
   Bibliography
Free Books by Charles River Editors
Discounted Books by Charles River Editors

## One of the Oldest Cities in the World

Byblos is located nearly 20 miles from Beirut on the Lebanese coast, bounded to the west by the Mediterranean Sea, to the north by the Taurus Mountains and Anatolia, to the east by the Lebanon and Anti-Lebanon mountain chains, and to the south and southeast by Israel and Syria. The Lebanon Mountains rise to a height of nearly 10,000 feet and closely straddle the coast, providing a series of promontories that enclosed sheltered bays and islands.[2] The Lebanese coast was formed by a number of geomorphologic processes, which produced conditions that were favorable for the development of ports and can be considered a key element in the rise of the seafaring people who settled there. Coastal erosion in the site of Byblos provided precisely this kind of landscape, with high cliffs backing gravelly and sandy coves. The shores are exposed to strong wind and waves, which over time eroded the limestone and conglomerate cliffs and produced the natural promontory and harbors that were later settled.

This was the historic crossroads between Europe, Asia, and Africa. Several great political and commercial centers of power developed on the coast, including Beirut, Tripoli, Sidon, and Tyre. They traded with inland towns such as Baalbek to exchange the valuable commodities that were available in the Lebanon and Anti-Lebanon mountain chains, the most precious of which were the forests of cedar woods that once grew there. In between these ranges was the fertile Beqaa Valley, which served as the primary farming landscape of the area throughout history.

Byblos has long held the reputation for being the most ancient city of the inhabited world–a status that is still supported by many experts and confirmed through archaeological studies. There are many legends associated with the foundation of the city, the most popular given by the Phoenician-Roman writer Philo of Byblos, who cited the Phoenician priest Sanchuniathon. According to this legend, Byblos was established by the titan Cronus as the first city on the Lebanese coast.[3] The evidence of tools found in caves along the coast of Lebanon shows that the region was certainly inhabited through the Paleolithic (ca. 50,000 BCE–10,000 BCE) to the Neolithic (ca. 10,000 BCE - 4,000 BCE) periods. The site of Byblos was visited by itinerant hunter-gatherer-fishers before it was settled in the Neolithic Era, as indicated by a small deposit of stone microliths and a notched arrowhead discovered there.[4] Carbon 14 dating has been used to support the hypothesis of its early inhabitation, with dates of up to 5700 BCE confirmed by charcoal samples at the site.[5]

Village life eventually formed as a result of the domestication of plants and animals during the Neolithic Era, and the oldest traces of human occupation on the site are those of a fishing village

---

[2] Brown, J. P. (1969) *The Lebanon and Phoenicia : ancient texts illustrating their physical geography and native industries*. Beirut: The American University of Beirut.
[3] Marcovich, M. (1996) "From Ishtar to Aphrodite." *Journal of Aesthetic Education*, 30(2), 43 - 59.
[4] Renfrew, C., Dixon, J. E., and Cann, J. R. (1966) "Obsidian and Early Cultural Contact in the Near East." *Proceedings of the Prehistoric Society (New Series)*, 32, 30 - 72.
[5] de Contenson, H. (1966) "Notes on the Chronology of Near Eastern Neolithic." *Bulletin of the American Schools of Oriental Research*, 184.

that was originally established on the promontory overlooking a natural harbor to the north. This inlet would eventually become the main port of Byblos, and it is still used to the present day. On the southern side of the promontory was a second bay with a sandy beach, which would have served as an ideal location to land ships before a manmade port could be constructed.[6] The promontory also featured two hills separated by a shallow valley, through which a natural spring ran.

**Marco Polis' panorama of the coastline at Byblos**

The first settlement at the site was established on the westernmost of these hills, first on the seaward-facing side and later spreading south into the valley, eventually covering an area of about 1.2 hectares.[7] Because of the steeply sloping topography the structures built on the hills had to be regularly leveled and reconstructed as they sunk towards the central depression, explaining why archaeologists have found evidence of so many phases of building activities.[8] This location allowed the earliest settlers at Byblos to fish, and archaeological evidence indicates that a great amount of fish were consumed at the site. It is likely that much of this was shore fishing, though the bones of some fish indicate that at least some of them were caught from boats at sea.[9]

Many traces of the lives of the earliest inhabitants of Byblos have been uncovered by archaeologists. There were up to 20 occupied structures in the village at a time, and

---

[6] Artin, G. (2010) "The necropolis and dwellings of Byblos during the Chalcolithic period: new interpretations." *Near Eastern Archaeology*, 73(2-3). 74 - 84.
[7] Jidéjian, N. (1968) *Byblos through the ages*. Beirut: Dar al Machreq.
[8] Sala, M. (2012) "Early and Middle Bronze Age Temples at Byblos: specificity and Levantine interconnections." In Khoury, S. E. (ed.) *Cult and Ritual on the Levantine Coast and its impact on the Eastern Mediterranean Realm: Proceedings of the International Symposium Beirut, 2012*. Beirut: Ministere de la Culture
[9] Potts, D. T. (2012) "Fish and Fishing." In Potts, D. T. (ed.) *A companion to the archaeology of the ancient Near East*. John Wiley & Sons. 220 - 235.

archaeological evidence indicates that the materials of old buildings were frequently recycled in the construction of new ones. These were circular plan huts with a single interior space, along with an exterior surrounded by a "garden" in which cereals and even reeds were grown.[10] Segmented sickles found at the site may have been used to harvest these plants.[11] The doorways faced the sun, which would have filled the space with light during the day. Their walls were made of stone up to 3 feet high, and presumably a material was used for the rest of the wall and ceiling that has since decomposed, such as timber or animal skins.[12] The floor was made of white lime plaster and small stones.

Several of the houses had interesting features, including small platforms that may have been used as hearths or altars, and mortars set into the floor to be used for grinding grain.[13] Furthermore, a great number of small finds were discovered in these huts, including flint spearheads, pestles, elliptical stone dishes (some with evidence of pigments), and ceramic jars that would have been used for storing food and liquids as well as to bury the dead.[14] Occasionally additional stone benches and small structures were added on to the huts, and over time they evolved to become rectangular in form, with high walls made entirely of stones.[15] The roof of these later huts would have been made of tree trunks and soil mixed with gravel–a method still used by some inhabitants of the Lebanese highlands. Chisels discovered at Byblos support environmental evidence that suggests the coastal plains and nearby mountains surrounding the site were covered in a dense forest during the Neolithic.[16]

A lot of evidence of Neolithic burial practices at the site has also been recovered by archaeologists. More than 30 burials have been found in the site, though many graves were surely demolished over time by the successive peoples who lived there.[17] The Neolithic population buried their dead in fetal positions on their left side in between the buildings of the settlement, and their children were buried in ceramic jars.[18] Some of these shallow burials contained grave goods, such as flint tools, polished stone axes, and ceramic objects.

Great quantities of ceramics were made in the site, and in a variety of shapes and sizes at that. Some of the more unique finds include baked clay spindle whorls, ceramic disks and rectangles, and clay stamp seals. There were two main types of ceramic vessels: rounded jars and hemispherical bowls. Some particularly large jars were supported by lugs and had handles fitted

---

[10] Nigro, L. (2007) "Aside the spring: Byblos and Jericho from village to town in the second half of the 4th millennium BC." *Byblos and Jericho in the Early Bronze I: Social Dynamics and Cultural Interactions*. Rome: Universit à di Rome: La Sapienza. 1 - 45.
[11] Moore, A. M. (1973) "The Late Neolithic in Palestine." *Levant*, 5(1). 36 - 68.
[12] Nigro, 2007
[13] Nigro, 2007
[14] Artin, 2010
[15] Nigro, 2007
[16] Renfrew, Dixon and Cann, 1966
[17] Dunand, M. (1973) *Byblos: Its History, Ruins and Legends*. Adrien-Maisonneuve.
[18] Dunand, 1973

onto their sides. They were made waterproof with a plaster of lime,[19] and many were decorated with incised patterns. Some even had impressions of local seashells across the surface.[20] Examples of ceramics decorated with cord markings have also been found there, though their scarcity suggests that these may have been brought to the site from another location.[21]

Bone tools may have also been used to decorate these vessels, or for a variety of other tasks. Many fishhooks made of goat and sheep bones have been found there, as well as beads and amulets.[22] A sheep's scapula was also discovered, decorated on one side with a series of incised lines, which may have been used as a musical instrument.[23]

Other objects found at the site were greenstone, steatite, and carnelian beads used as objects of adornment. Sea shells may have also been used for this purpose. Small greenstone human and animal figurines were also discovered there, though their function is unknown.[24]

At this point in time it is unclear whether Byblos was involved in maritime trade with other coastal sites in the region, such as at Ugarit in northern Syria, or even with Egypt. Historians are uncertain of these trade links because many of the resources used in the site could have been acquired locally. The flint used to make the sickle blades, arrowheads, axes, and chisels may have been obtained from the beds of nearby river valleys, such as the Wadi Deir Banat south of Byblos where flint deposits lie exposed to the open air.[25] Limestone, granite, greenstone, sandstone, and basalt were also available in the coastal region. Conversely, some resources were evidently brought from distant lands, indicating that some amount of trade and exchange may have taken place at this point in history; for example, spectrographic analysis of obsidian objects found at Byblos has shown that these originated from Anatolia.[26]

From the 3rd millennium BCE, the first evidence of streets and temples appear at Byblos. The first signs of a proper city can be observed from this time, with evidence of a standardized form of home construction, organized religion, and a stratified social hierarchy. In fact, the religious architecture of Bronze Age Byblos provides a fascinating illustration of practices that were later adopted by the Phoenicians. The two major temple complexes of the Early Bronze Age city were the L-shaped Temple and the Temple of Ba'alat Gebal, built in approximately 2700 BCE. There were many other temples built during this time, including the *Enceinte Sacrée, Chapelle Orientale*, Southeast Temple, *Temple a Escalier*, and the *Sanctuaire méridional*–all names given to the sites by the French archaeologists of the early 20th century.[27] Most of these remained in

---

[19] Miller, R. (1980). Water use in Syria and Palestine from the Neolithic to the Bronze Age. *World Archaeology, 11*(3), 331-341.
[20] Dunand, 1973
[21] Moore, A. M. T. (1978) *The Neolithic of the Levant*. Oxford: University of Oxford
[22] Moore, 1978
[23] Moore, 1978
[24] Dunand, 1973
[25] Moore, 1978
[26] Moore, 1978

use in the Middle Bronze Age, and at least the main structures were still in use until the Hellenistic-Roman period.

The center of the town was reserved for these religious buildings. They were focused around a built up sacred well in the center of the depression between the two hills of the peninsula, and drew upon the natural stream there.[28] It was this spring that functioned as the focus of religious life in the village, its life-giving waters playing a central role in the rise of the city.[29] Other contemporary settlements showed a similar process, as religious cults at Tyre, Sidon, and Arwad were established near water sources. The temples were built on artificial terraces and podiums, though these did little to allay the effects of the steep slope upon which they were built over the long term. For this reason, most of the temples had to be rebuilt a number of times during the phases of their use.[30]

The Phoenicians and their predecessors worshiped a number of Near Eastern and Mesopotamian deities that were later identified with the Greek and Roman pantheon. A great number of deities existed in their pantheon, many of them corresponding with the ancient Semitic religions of Mesopotamia, and much like in Mesopotamia each god or goddess was frequently linked to a city. Although their earliest names are unknown, they later became known as Melqart, the god of storms and mythical ruler of Tyre; Astarte, who was worshiped throughout the Near East; Baal Hammon, the god of weather and fertility, whose cult was chiefly worshiped in Carthage; and Eshmun, the tutelary god of Sidon, worshiped for his healing abilities.

Thanks to its long relationship with Egypt, Byblos also assimilated some of the religious traditions of the Egyptian pantheon. The city became a religious center for the cult of Osiris, and later it developed into an important place of worship for the Canaanite god Resheph, god of plague and war. It is believed that his cult was introduced to Byblos from New Kingdom Egypt (1540–1080 BCE), where he served as god of horses and chariots and acquired particular popularity during the Ramesside period (1292–1069 BCE).[31]

The most important deity at Byblos was Ba'alat Gebal, the so-called "Lady of Byblos". She was identified by the ancient Phoenician priest Sanchuniathon as the sister of Astarte, and also as the Titan Dione, who was the mother of the Hellenistic goddess of love and fertility, Aphrodite.[32] Because of her importance, the temple of Ba'alat Gebal was the main religious complex of the city. It was dedicated to the tutelary goddess of the city, and for this reason it likely had a key

---

[27] Sala, 2012
[28] Sala, 2012
[29] The well itself remained in use for millennia, used until the 1930s when it was known as the "Ain el Meleek".
[30] Saghieh, M. S. (1975) *Byblos in the 3rd millennium: A Reconstruction of the Stratigraphy and a Study of the Cultural Connections.* London: University of London Doctoral Dissertations
[31] Münnich, M. M. (2013) *The God Resheph in the Ancient Near East.* Mohr Siebeck.
[32] Espinel, A. D. (2002) "The Role of the Temple of Ba'alat Gebal as Intermediary between Egypt and Byblos during the Old Kingdom." *Studien zur altägyptischen Kultur.* 103 - 119.

role in the political and commercial relations between the city's hierarchy and with its neighbors, including the Egyptians.[33] Within the temple ceramic fragments with hieroglyphs were found, indicating that they had been left to the goddess of Byblos by the Egyptian pharaohs Cheops, Mycerinus, Sahure, Unas, Pepi and Khasekemoui.[34]

The origins of the sanctuary lie as far back as the second half of the 3rd millennium BCE, and over time it grew north and west of the sacred spring in the center of the town. It was a large complex divided into a number of wings. To the north was a courtyard surrounded by rooms and containing the main cult shrine. A second large courtyard was to the south surrounded by additional auxiliary rooms. Access to the complex was via a stone staircase leading from a triangular forecourt to the east. The various parts of the building were demolished and rebuilt frequently, and over time the temple developed two large pillared halls (or unroofed open spaces) and a separate northern section.[35]

The L-Shaped Temple was one of the longest lasting active religious sites at Byblos and was probably also dedicated to Ba'alat Gebal.[36] The complex was composed of a sacred precinct, a forecourt, and two auxiliary sections to the northeast and west which may have been used as accommodation for the priests and also as ceremonial spaces. The precinct was the core of the complex, square in form with three chapels in the center. Two enormous obelisks were erected in the L-Shaped Temple–the earliest example of a practice that reached its peak with the Temple of Obelisks (which later occupied the same site). The use of obelisks, or betyls, was a practice that likely originated in Syria (where they are known as *massebot*), but it may have also come from Pharaonic Egypt.[37] This site continued to be an active religious complex until well into the Hellenistic period.

The other temples in the city are no less remarkable. The *Enceinte Sacrée* is the earliest religious sanctuary of Byblos, located to the west of the sacred spring and dating from as far back as the 4th millennium BCE. A temple building was constructed there in approximately 3300 BCE. Although it was in a poor state of preservation when archaeologists discovered it in the 20th century, the general form of the complex has be reconstructed: it was divided from the Bronze Age village by a curved boundary wall supported by stone buttresses, and access was along a stone paved street–likely one of the earliest in the settlement.[38] The temple itself was a rectangular *cella* with its main entrance on the eastern wall–that is, facing the well at the center of the religious landscape. This temple remained in use throughout the period of transition in which the small village developed into a town, during which time it was reconstructed using new building techniques. The main additions were an inner partition wall and a new path leading to

---

[33] Espinel, 2002
[34] Espinel, 2002
[35] Sala, 2012
[36] Sala, 2012
[37] Graesser, C. F. (1972) "Standing stones in ancient Palestine." *The Biblical Archaeologist, 35*(2). 34 - 63.
[38] Saghieh, 1975

the central well. Over time the structure was rebuilt in an oval form and additional rooms were added, until it settled into its final form: a rectangular temple enclosure surrounded by auxiliary chapels, with a large square *cella* containing the shrine.[39]

In 2150, the Amorites invaded Byblos and put a temporary end to its growth. They destroyed the temple of Ba'alat Gebal, though it was later reconstructed. The L-shaped temple was also destroyed during this incursion, and in its place the Temple of the Obelisks was later erected. The Temple of the Obelisks contained a raised podium with the main shrine and a lower courtyard filled with over 40 obelisks and other standing stones in various shapes and sizes.[40] Following the Amorite invasion a monumental staircase was built at the *Enceinte Sacrée*, and during this period of reconstruction a new temple complex was established, the *Temple a Escalier*. This consisted of a massive stone building built upon a tall podium, which resembled the form of "tower temples" that spread across the region from Syria during the early 2nd millennium BCE, but it differed insofar as it made use of architectural features found only in the coastal Levant, such as Ugarit.[41]

There was a notable shift in the religious landscape after the Amorite invasion. For example, there was a widespread effort to renovate open-air cult places, which indicates that the entire population of the town became increasingly involved in collective rites and ceremonies.[42] This phenomenon occurred elsewhere in the Levant at the same time, reflecting the gradual development of a shared system of religious beliefs and practices across the region. During this time, all of the temples surrounding the sacred well were connected by a concentric road which was linked to the wider infrastructure of streets that was developed in the city.[43] This allowed a greater number of worshippers to move between the different religious complexes, and may indicate a growth in pilgrimage and religious processions during festivals at this site.

---

[39] Sala, 2012
[40] Saghieh, 1975
[41] Sala, 2012
[42] Sala, 2012
[43] Sala, 2012

## An Egyptian Vassal

**A Terracotta jug from the Bronze Age found at Byblos**

Following the invasion of the Amorites in 2150 BCE, the town became a place of international trade, in particular between Mesopotamia and Egypt, and from this point until the Hellenistic period, the settlement was known as Gubla. The first ruler of which historians have knowledge is Ibdadi (ca. 2050 BCE), who is mentioned in the cuneiform texts of Drehem, a temple suburb in the Sumerian city of Nippur.[44] He is described varyingly as leader, lord, or king of Byblos, but in general, according to documentary evidence from Egypt, the highest rank in the settlement was "mayor" until Byblos became an independent city-state with its own king in the 1st millennium BCE.[45] It is unclear what the precise relationship between pre-Phoenician Byblos and Egypt

---

[44] Botterweck, G. J., and Ringgren, H. (2004) *Theological dictionary of the Old Testament*. Grand Rapids: William. B. Eerdmans Publishing.

entailed, namely whether the city was officially an Egyptian domain and its mayors simply governed it on behalf of the Pharaoh, or if instead they accepted titles bestowed on them by the Egyptians simply because they reflected pre-existing power structures.[46]

The city became even more closely connected with the fate of Egypt during the 2nd millennium BCE. The earliest artistic representations of the Phoenicians have been found in a damaged relief at Memphis, dating from the time of the Egyptian Fourth Dynasty (2613–2494 BCE) and depicting the arrival of an Asiatic princess to be the pharaoh's bride. She is escorted by a fleet of ships, probably of a type known to the Egyptians as "Byblos ships", and their crews were evidently Phoenicians.[47]

One story associated with the site dating from this period is the journey of Wenamun. Although considered a factual account of a journey that did take place, the general consensus in the present day is that this is a work of fiction written by someone who never actually visited Byblos. Nonetheless, the tale gives a unique perspective into the early relations between Egypt and Byblos. It tells of a priest in Thebes who struggles to acquire cedar wood for the construction of a sacred ship to be dedicated to Amon.[48] He was sent by the Pharaoh to the Levant to purchase this timber from the people of Byblos, bringing with him valuable linen, oil, and other valuable Egyptian commodities, but upon arriving at Byblos he was mugged and imprisoned.

Regardless of the fate of Wenamun, Egyptian monuments and inscriptions found in Byblos do indicate strong diplomatic and commercial relations existed between the two powers throughout the latter half of the 2nd millennium BCE. Costly gifts were given by the pharaohs to the mayors of the city, and the natural harbors of Byblos were used for the construction of Egyptian-style *kebenit* ships.[49] These ships were capable of sailing and rowing across oceans and rivers, which gave them an advantage over many of their competitors, and some were even fitted with rams. The chief goddess of the city, Ba'alat Gebal, was also being worshiped in Egypt by the Egyptian 12th Dynasty (1991–1803 BCE).[50]

After the life of Ibdadi, there followed a long period in which almost nothing is known of the city until the reign of Abishemu I (1820–1795 BCE). Most of the knowledge of Abishemu I

---

[45] Ben-Tor, D. (2007) "Scarabs of Middle Bronze age rulers of Byblos." In Bickel, S., Schroer, S., Schurte, R., and Uehlinger, C. (eds) *Bilder als Quellen. Images as Sources. Studies on ancient Near Eastern artefacts and the Bible inspired by the work of Othmar Keel*. Academic Press Fribourg Vandenhoeck & Ruprecht Göttingen. 177 - 188

[46] Ben-Tor, Daphna, 2003, "Egyptian-Levantine Relations and Chronology in the Middle Bronze Age: Scarab Research". In Bietak, M. (ed.) *The Synchronisation of Civilisations in The Eastern Mediterranean in the 2nd millennium B.C. II*. Vienna: Österreichische Akademie der Wissenschaften, Denkschriften der Gesamtakademie. 239 - 48

[47] Bagnall, R. S. (2011) *The Oxford Handbook of Papyrology*. Oxford: Oxford University Press

[48] Egberts, A. (1991) "The Chronology of 'The Report of Wenamun'". *The Journal of Egyptian Archaeology*, 57 - 67.

[49] Maiseis, C. (1997) *Early civilizations of the Old World*. London: Routledge

[50] Espinel, 2002

comes from evidence recovered at his tomb in the necropolis at Byblos,[51] because fortunately, his tomb was for the most part untouched when it was discovered by archaeologists in the 20th century and still contained a treasure trove of valuable objects. In the burial chamber was a white limestone sarcophagus of the mayor, and among the artifacts recovered were a beautiful ceramic pot, weapons plated with gold, gold jewelry, obsidian vases inscribed with the name of the Egyptian king Amenemhat III (1843–1797 BCE), and a silver vase that may have come from the Aegean region.[52] The rich grave goods bear testimony to the strong influence Egypt had on Byblos from this early period–indeed, some believe that the Egyptian writing system was used in the city during this time.[53] The existence of Abishemu I is also known by an Egyptian cylinder seal.[54] Interestingly, no bones of the king were present in the tomb, and the name of Abishemu I was not found within the burial chamber itself, but it appeared in an adjacent corridor that linked the grave with that of his son and successor, Ipshemouabi.[55]

Ipshemouabi reigned over Byblos between 1795 and 1780 BCE. His tomb was also discovered at the necropolis of Byblos and, like that of his father, it was relatively untouched.[56] It also contained a staggering number of valuable objects, so much so that it appears to have been far richer than that of Abishemu I. He was also buried in a sarcophagus of white limestone, and many of the objects found in the burial chamber resembled those present in the tomb of Abishemu I, but in far greater quantities. They continue to reflect the influence of Egypt; amongst the most notable grave goods was a breastplate with an obsidian stone inscribed with the name of the Egyptian king Amenemhat IV (1797–1787 BCE) and a shell-shaped pendant with the image of a hawk.[57] The mayor was named on two objects found in the tomb, which explicitly label him as the son of Abishemu I.[58]

Ipshemouabi was succeeded by Cain (1780–1770 BCE), who was perhaps his son. His identity is known only through inscribed cylinder seals, and according to clay tablets found in the Syrian city of Mari, Cain was followed by Reyen (1770–1765 BCE), who was succeeded by his son Yattin (1765–1735 BCE).[59] Yattin was succeeded by Abishemu II (1735–1700 BCE), who ruled over Byblos during the same period as the great Babylonian king Hammurabi (1792–1750 BCE). The city appears to have had close relations with Mari during this time, as the tablets also attest

---

[51] Schiestl, R. (2007) "The Coffin from Tomb I at Byblos." *Ägypten und Levante/Egypt and the Levant, 17*, 265 - 271.
[52] Schiestl, 2007
[53] Daniels, P. T. (1996) "The first civilizations." In Daniels, P. T., and Bright, W. (eds) *The world's writing systems*. Oxford: Oxford University Press on Demand. 21 - 32.
[54] Teissier, B. (1996) *Egyptian iconography on Syro-Palestinian cylinder seals of the Middle Bronze Age* . Saint-Paul.
[55] Schiestl, 2007
[56] Schiestl, 2007
[57] Bevan, A. (2007) *Stone vessels and values in the Bronze Age Mediterranean*. Cambridge: Cambridge University Press.
[58] Schiestl, 2007
[59] Oppenheim, A. L. (Ed.). (1967) *Letters from Mesopotamia: Official business, and private letters on clay tablets from two millennia*. Chicago: University of Chicago Press.

that many embroidered garments and carpets were imported from the city in the Euphrates valley.[60] It was perhaps due to the rumors of Hammurabi's campaigns throughout the north of Mesopotamia–and eventual capture of Mari–that Abishemu II formed a pact of allegiance with the Egyptian king Neferhotep I.[61]

Abishemu II was succeeded by Yapa-Shemouabi (1700–1690 BCE), and after him, his son Akery (1690–1670) came to power. During the rule of Akery, the city was attacked by another people, the Hyksos, who went on to conquer Egypt and establish the 15th Dynasty of Egypt.[62] Byblos was subsequently liberated by Tyre, but the city continued to share close relations with Egypt.[63] One of the most impressive sites in Byblos dates from this period: the Temple of the Obelisks. Located within a sacred enclosure, which was reached via a large courtyard, the temple was focused around a great symbolic obelisk around which many smaller obelisks were arranged.[64] The courtyard was framed by a number of cultic facilities and workshops which produced votive offerings for the temple, the most spectacular of which was a series of bronze statues covered in gold leaf. They also manufactured golden ceremonial axes with filigree decorations, and terra cotta objects.[65]

---

[60] Kitchen, K. A. (1967) "Byblos, Egypt, and Mari in the Early 2nd millennium BC." *Orientalia*, 36(1). 39 - 54.
[61] Kitchen, 1967
[62] Albright, W. F. (1965) "Further light on the history of Middle-Bronze Byblos." *Bulletin of the American Schools of Oriental Research*, 179. 38 - 43.
[63] Albright, 1965
[64] Sala, 2012
[65] Sala, 2012

## Pictures of the Temple of the Obelisks

Once again, there followed an extensive period in which little is known of the events at Byblos until the invasion of Canaan and Syria by the Egyptian pharaoh Thutmose III (18th Dynasty, r. 1479–1425 BCE) that took place between 1460 and 1455 BCE.[66] In letters to Tell el-Amarna from the time of Pharaoh Amenhotep IV (1351–1334 BCE), the Phoenicians are identified as the *Kenaani* or *Kinaani* (Canaanites). The letters also note that at the time, the city of Byblos was ruled by mayor Rib-Addi.

**A statue of Thutmose III**

Rib-Addi came to power as ruler of Byblos in approximately 1375 BCE as a vassal and protectorate of the Egyptian empire, and a number of interesting vignettes into the rule of Rib-Addi are provided by the Amarna letters. For example, in one of the letters he begged the

---

[66] Redford, D. B. (2003) *The Wars in Syria and Palestine of Thutmose III*. Brill.

Egyptian pharaoh to intervene in a dispute with Hing Ammunira of Beirut over the capture of two merchants ships from Byblos. In another, he complained of an attack by the Egyptian commissioner Pihuri that killed a number of inhabitants of Byblos. He also poignantly wrote of his fear of rebellion, perhaps referring to a coup d'état that occurred in Tyre during which his parents, sister, and daughters were killed.[67]

In another letter, Rib-Addi wrote of an assassination attempt organized by Abdi Ashirta (1385–1344), king of the Amurru.[68] Amurru was a small independent kingdom in central Syria centered on the cities of Tell Hazor and Ebla, and the people of Amurru had allied themselves with Tudhaliya III, emperor of the Hittites. Together, their combined forces presented a key threat to not only Byblos, but Egypt as well.[69] For this reason, Abdi-Ashirta was kidnapped and murdered by Egyptian troops under the orders of Pharaoh Amenhotep IV, but this did not stop the Amurru plot.

As it turned out, the new king, Aziru, was just as unscrupulous as his predecessor. Barely in office, he started a campaign to restore the authority of his father over the region. Although nominally a vassal to the Egyptians by treaty, Aziru conquered a number of cities along the Mediterranean coastline north of Byblos, including Ardata (which he made his capital), Irqata, and Phoenician Tripoli. He established alliances with King Niqmaddou II of Ugarit and King Etakkama of Kadesh (though the latter eventually betrayed him and joined the Hittites).[70]

The conquests of Aziru worried his neighbors, especially Rib-Addi, who was directly responsible for the death of Abdi Ashirta, father of Aziru. Rib-Addi was exiled to Beirut by his younger brother, Ilirabih, for a period of four months.[71] However, he received word that in his absence Ilirabih had been dethroned, after which Rib-Addi appealed to Pharaoh Amenhotep IV to help reinstate him as ruler of Byblos. As he was formally a vassal of Egypt, Aziru was ordered by the pharaoh to lend aid to Rib-Addi, but he betrayed the mission and gave Rib-Addi over to the leaders of Sidon, where he was killed.[72]

Aziru subsequently proclaimed himself king of Byblos, and despite the fact Amenhotep IV ordered him to come to Egypt to explain his actions, within a year he was allowed to return to Phoenicia to face the threat of the advancing Hittite armies.[73] Once he had returned to the relative safety of Byblos, Aziru contacted Suppiluliuma, king of the Hittites, and offered to

---

[67] Artzi, P. (1964) "Vox Populi in the El-Amarna Tablets", *Revue d'Assyriologie et d'archéologie orientale*, 58(4). 159 - 166.
[68] Mendenhall, G. E. (1947) "The Message of Abdi-Ashirta to the Warriors, EA 74." *Journal of Near Eastern Studies*, 6(2). 123 - 124.
[69] Artzi, 1964
[70] Artzi, 1964
[71] Reviv, H. (1969) "On urban representative institutions and self-government in Syria-Palestine in the second half of the 2nd millennium BC." *Journal of the Economic and Social History of the Orient*, 12(1). 283 - 297.
[72] Reviv, 1969
[73] Liverani, M. (2004) "Aziru, servant of two masters." *Myth and Politics in Ancient Near Eastern Historiography*. Sheffield: Equinox Publishing. 125 - 144.

switch allegiances. Byblos thus came under the rule of the Hittites, and during this time the city was ruled by two kings of whom little is known: Ari-Teshub (1338–1336 BCE) and Tuppi-Teshub (1290–1280 BCE).[74] Tuppi-Teshub evidently helped the Hittites suppress the rebellion of King Tette of Nuhashshe (near present-day Aleppo) and King Etakkama of Kadesh.[75] His sister, Ahatmilki, became the wife of King Niqmepa of Ugarit.

**A statue of Amenhotep IV in the Egyptian Museum in Cairo**

---

[74] Jidéjian, 1968
[75] Elgavish, D. (2004) "Extradition of Fugitives in International Relations in the Ancient Near East." In *Jewish Law Association Studies XIV: The Jerusalem 2002 Conference Volume*. 33 - 58.

## The Phoenicians

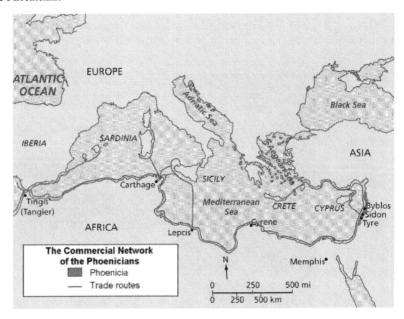

**A map of Phoenicia and Phoenician trade routes**

Since the Phoenicians never developed a historiographical tradition like that of the Egyptians and Mesopotamians, determining their origins is problematic at best and can only be approached through a combination of philology, historiography, and archaeology. Of course, it must also be remembered that when scholars analyze the historical texts of other peoples who wrote about the Phoenicians, they have to keep in mind that foreign writers likely had biases about the people they were describing.

Nowhere is this concept more apparent than in the Bible, thanks to two verses from the Old Testament that cast the Phoenicians in a negative light: "And Ahab the son of Omri did evil in the sight of the Lord above all that were before him. And it came to pass, as if it had been a light thing for him to walk in the sins of Jeroboam the son of Nebat, that he took to wife Jezebel the daughter of Ethba'al king of the Sidonians, and went and served Ba'al, and worshiped him" (1 Kings 16: 30-31). Unfortunately, these two verses have been used throughout history to depict the Phoenicians as licentious heathens, when the reality is that many other Biblical verses depict the Phoenicians as being quite adept in the arts of ancient statecraft and oftentimes allies of the Israelites (as will be discussed further below).

Another ancient historical source that is questionable in its accuracy of Phoenician origins (but not as biased) comes from the 5th century BCE Greek historian Herodotus. In his seminal *Histories*, Herodotus wrote, "These people came originally from the so-called Red Sea: and as soon as they had penetrated to the Mediterranean and settled in the country where they are today, they took to making long trading voyages. Loaded with Egyptian and Assyrian goods, they called at various places along the coast including Argos, in those days the most important place in the land now called Hellas" (Herodotus, *Histories*, I, 1). Although most scholars discount the Red Sea origins of the Phoenicians, who occupied the Levantine coast of the Mediterranean Sea during ancient times, Herodotus' account of Phoenician trade and colonization can be corroborated by multiple primary sources.

**A bust depicting Herodotus**

Today, scholars believe that the origins of the Phoenician people can be traced closer to their homeland of Phoenicia, and they have generally used the ancient Phoenician language as a way to determine the ancient civilization's origins. The ancient Phoenician language was Semitic and very closely related to Hebrew and Aramaic, which were the other two major ancient Semitic languages of the Levant (Moscati 1968, 91), and due to the linguistic similarities, scholars believe that the Phoenicians shared a common ancestry with the Hebrews and they were both known as Canaanites before they became Phoenicians and Israelites (Markoe 2000, 10).

Although philology has allowed the linguistic origins of the Phoenicians to be unlocked, their geographic origins will continue to be debated until more conclusive archeological evidence is discovered. The Phoenician culture owed much of its historic importance to the varied characteristics of the landscape that was their homeland. Sometimes arid and sometimes incredibly lush and fertile, the territory was a mosaic of varying landscapes. This sliver of country teeters between the two mountain ranges that run in parallel to the coast, rich in natural resources and freshwater springs.[76] Lebanon's flora was an essential element to its patrimony, and in particular that which was found in the mountain regions. Mount Lebanon is the westernmost range, reaching over three thousand meters above sea level at its highest peak. The mountain chain was once richly forested in cedar woods. This range is faced by the Anti-Lebanon Chain to the east, which reaches a maximum height of a little over two thousand eight hundred meters above sea level along the border between Lebanon and Syria. The fertile Beqaa Valley is nestled between these two ranges, where a whole range of cereals were cultivated from ancient times.

The modern discovery and study of the ancient Phoenicians did not begin in earnest until 1860, when Emperor Napoleon III of France led a punitive military expedition into Lebanon against members of the Islamic Druze sect, which had just massacred members of the Maronite Christian sect (Herm 1975, 27). Perhaps inspired by his grandfather, Napoleon Bonaparte, who led both French troops and scholars into Egypt in 1799, Napoleon III brought his own scholars, namely Ernest Renan, to study the ancient ruins of the cities of coastal Lebanon (Herm 1975, 27).

---

[76] Brown, J. P. (1969) *The Lebanon and Phoenicia: ancient texts illustrating their physical geography and native industries*. Beirut: The American University of Beirut.

**Ernest Renan**

Unlike Egypt, which has a number of intact ancient monuments for scholars to study (especially in Upper Egypt), the major ancient Phoenician cities had been thoroughly built over in medieval and modern times, but this problem did not deter Renan, and his efforts later drew other renowned historians and archaeologists to Lebanon. After World War I, when Lebanon was briefly ruled by the French under a League of Nations mandate, more scholars traveled there in order to try to unlock the mysteries of Phoenicia, and the most famous early 20th century scholar to study the ancient Phoenician ruins was the esteemed French Egyptologist Pierre Montet, who used his knowledge of ancient history and modern archeological techniques to uncover some monuments from Byblos (Herm 1975, 29).

**Pierre Montet**

Although World War II and modern development hampered extensive archaeological expeditions of the major Phoenician cities, Renan and Montet's early efforts helped to open Phoenician history to the modern world. It was soon revealed that the three cities of Byblos, Tyre, and Sidon were the backbone of ancient Phoenician culture. Most of the ancient Phoenician cities were located along the coastline of what are today the modern nation nations of Israel and Lebanon, with Byblos being the farthest to the north, Tyre at the south end, and Sidon between the two.

According to the ancient Greek historian Herodotus, Phoenician cities had been founded so long ago that a thriving cult of Herakles existed in Tyre by at least 2750 BCE.[77] Ancient Egyptian stories tell of a group of "sea peoples" that invaded the Levant around 1200 BCE, who were believed to have mixed with the Canaanites and created the Phoenician culture.[78] Historians still debate how much of an impact these "sea peoples" had on the development of the Phoenicians as the greatest sailors in the Mediterranean, because archaeological evidence shows that the Phoenicians already had a special connection to the sea, trading and travelling as far back as the 2nd millennium BCE. The Canaanites are a people mentioned in the Old Testament as living throughout the Levant from approximately 2000-1200 BCE. Since they precede the Phoenicians, and because their homelands overlap, it has been frequently assumed that the

---

[77] Mikalson, J. D. (2004) *Herodotus and Religion in the Persian Wars*. Chapel Hill: The University of North Carolina Press.
[78] D'Amato R., and Salimbeti, A. (2015) *The Sea Peoples of the Mediterranean Bronze Age 1450–1100 BC*. London: Osprey

Canaanites and the Phoenicians were the same people. The archaeological remains of the Phoenicians indicate that they developed steadily out of the older Canaanite cultures, but it is unclear how much genetic continuity there was.

Some of the things that made the Phoenicians so enigmatic were their fluid political boundaries and the role they had as conduits of the different cultures that existed around the Mediterranean world. "Phoenicia" was not a clearly demarcated and unified kingdom, with borders that separated it from its neighbors. Instead, it was a culture spread throughout a string of city states across the Mediterranean and beyond. To support their trade and travel the Phoenicians founded colonies with harbors and warehouses as ports of call, which served to break up the long journeys away from their homeland. Between 1200 BCE and 800 BCE the Phoenicians engaged in their first wave of colonization, during which they established trading posts at key locations around the Mediterranean, including those at Utica in 1101 BCE and at Carthage in 814 BCE. Between 800 BCE and 600 BCE, these trading posts started becoming full colonies, and over time some would eventually surpass their mother cities in wealth and power.

To get a sense of the extent of the Phoenician sphere of influence, it is useful to imagine being on a vessel setting off from their coastline on a journey that will go around the Mediterranean and beyond. Such a journey began in the Phoenician mainland. The building block of their civilization and trade was the cedar wood of Lebanon, an excellent timber that was used to build sturdy cargo vessels and warships. After building the ships, the Phoenicians then used those ships to transport cedar to other powers in the Mediterranean world. 3,000 years ago the Mount Lebanon range was covered in cedar forests, and the timber was primarily traded through Baalbek, situated in the Anti-Lebanon Mountains.

Seafaring merchants were evidently free to go where the market and winds took them. Travelling along the northern coasts of the Mediterranean, Phoenician traders would have stopped at their colony of Motya, in present-day Sicily. A bronze statue was recovered there in 1979 known as the Youth of Motya. The form of this figure is said to resemble the Tyrian deity Melqart, indicating that cross-cultural exchanges were taking place between Phoenicia and Motya by approximately 480 to 450 BCE.[79]

Then they traveled on to their rich colonies at Majorca and Sardinia. Without gold deposits of their own, the Sardinians must have acquired this commodity from the Phoenician traders. The forms of some of the rings and amulets found there indicate that the Phoenicians themselves worked the gold in the colonies, creating them according to standardized designs in small molds.[80] In return, the Phoenicians acquired glass ointment jars, necklaces, and amulets.

The commanders of the Phoenician fleets had to have many skills. Not only did they have to

---

[79] Papadopoulos, J. K. (2014) "The Motya Youth: Apollo Karneios, Art, and Tyranny in the Greek West." *The Art Bulletin*, 96: 4. 395 - 423

[80] Neville, A. (2007) *Mountains of Silver and Rivers of Gold: The Phoenicians in Iberia*. Oxford: Oxbow Books

have an expert knowledge of the Mediterranean Sea and foreign lands, they also had to know the art of trading between diverse cultures as well. Many scholars believe that Phoenicians were amongst the earliest people to identify the North Star and use it to navigate during their voyages.[81] For years scholars speculated as to how the Phoenicians managed to communicate with each other on their voyages, and how they organized the complex trade of such a variety of goods. It was the discovery of the sarcophagus of the Phoenician king Ahiram, which dates to the 13th century BCE, that helped archaeologists understand their great organizational skills. Engraved in the sarcophagus is a bas relief-image and one of only five known examples of inscriptions from the language of the Phoenician city of Byblos.[82] The Phoenicians developed a phonetic alphabet that influenced the way that people write today; Europa, sister of Cadmos of Tyre, was a historical figure that allegedly introduced the alphabet to the Greeks, who copied and adapted it before the Romans further developed it into the Latin script that the West uses today.

In addition to being outstanding sailors, the Phoenicians were famed shipbuilders. They mass-produced ships, and could replace lost vessels with great speed. At the shipyards of Carthage, all of the parts of their ships were clearly marked by different letters or symbols, and kept ready for quick assembly.[83] However, crossing the seas was no easy matter, even with the help of a good ship, and help from the gods was sought during their voyages across the Mediterranean.

By approximately 1100 BCE the Phoenicians had reached the western gateway of the Mediterranean, beyond the Pillars of Hercules at the isthmus of Gibraltar and south along the Atlantic beaches of Africa between Morocco and Guinea. The Pillars of Hercules were known by the Phoenicians as the Pillars of Melqart, named after their primary deity, the god of storms and mythical ruler of Tyre.[84] The Phoenicians were some of the only Mediterranean cultures brave enough to venture into the Atlantic; many others believed that beyond the Pillars of Hercules was nothing more than the edge of the world.

---

[81] Marston, E. (2001) *The Phoenicians*. Singapore: Marshall Cavendish
[82] Vance, D. R. (1994) "Literary Sources for the History of Palestine and Syria: The Phœnician Inscriptions." *The Biblical Archaeologist*, 57:1. 2 – 19
[83] Woodman, 2012
[84] Bonanno, A. (1986) *Archaeology and Fertility Cult in the Ancient Mediterranean: Papers Presented at the First International Conference on Archaeology of the Ancient Mediterranean, University of Malta, 2-5 September 1985*. Amsterdam: B. R. Grüner Publishing Co.

**The Pillars of Hercules (European in the foreground and North African in the background)**

To reckon with the hazards of venturing so far the Phoenicians struck a spiritual bargain with their gods. At Gorham's Cave, located at the base of the Rock of Gibraltar, archaeologists have discovered many thousands of talismans, rings, amulets and other finely crafted tiny items that are believed to have been deposited there by passing Phoenicians as votive offerings to create an alliance with their deities.[85]

---

[85] Moscati, S. (2001) *The Phoenicians*. New York: I. B. Taurus

**Gorham's Cave**

Arriving in Africa, the Phoenicians would lay out their wares on the beach before returning to their ships and sending up massive plumes of smoke. Local communities would see the smoke and place the gold they were offering in exchange beside the merchandise before withdrawing with their goods.[86] African cultures were very taken with the goods from the east, which was so different from the yellow metal that was found in abundance there. This was the great bargain of the Phoenicians, and it's indicative of their shrewdness as traders, leaving inexpensive pottery and jewelry before returning home with precious commodities.

Excavations in England have revealed that the Phoenicians may have reached even these far-off lands.[87] There they traded for skins, but tin seems to have been the major commodity sought there by the Phoenicians, as it was in great demand in the eastern Mediterranean for producing bronze and other alloys. These voyages in the storms of the North Atlantic always held the portent of danger, and according to wall-reliefs found in the Near East the brave Phoenician captains may have safeguarded their ships and cargoes by tying themselves to the bow, so that they could see more clearly and avoid cliffs and rocky shoals.[88] If they made it, the returning ships would almost always stop off at the Phoenician colony of Cadiz (present-day Spain), where they would trade for iron.[89]

---

[86] Moscati, 2001
[87] Ball, W. (2010) Out of Arabia: Phoenicians, Arabs, and the Discovery of Europe. Northampton: Olive Branch Press
[88] Woodman, R. (2012) *The History of the Ship: The Comprehensive story of seafaring from the earliest times to the present day.* Bloomsbury Publishing

On their way home along the southern Mediterranean the Phoenician merchants would have stopped at their colony of Carthage, which had been founded in the late 9th century BCE as the Phoenicians extended their reach across the Mediterranean. From its roots the colony grew to dominate the region, eventually surpassing the power of its founders. Their ships might also have sailed up the Nile to Memphis and the kingdoms of the pharaohs. Their presence is indicated by a foreign quarter called the "Tyrian Camp" located a short distance south of the temple of Hephaestus in Memphis.[90] The Egyptian pharaohs treasured cedar for its fragrant resin, and the Phoenicians would have traded this wood for linen–a hard-wearing fabric that only the Egyptians knew how to make. This material was indispensable for the robust sails used on Phoenician ships. Egyptian amulets were also greatly valued by the Phoenicians because of the magical powers they were believed to possess.[91] Two kings of the Phoenician city of Sidon, Tabnit and his son Eshmunazar II, were buried in Egyptian sarcophagi complete with Phoenician inscriptions, and they were even mummified in the Egyptian style.

Finally, Phoenician traders completed the loop by returning to the Phoenician mainland. There, they could turn their commercial interest to the East, where they sold their commodities to the Persians and to their fellow countrymen. They would be left with a whole lot more wealth than they used to pay for the original cedar in Baalbek. But what was it that pushed the Phoenicians so far across the sea? It was gold. The Phoenicians existed at the edge of great land-based empires that were constantly exacting tribute from them. This served as a major push-factor, as they had to acquire wealth to make these payments (the pull factor being that they could also make great wealth for themselves). The easiest way for the Phoenicians to increase their prosperity was by contact with other peoples, and the quickest route to new lands and new cultures was across the Mediterranean. Therefore, they became outstanding sailors and astute traders.

While sailing beyond the Straits of Gibraltar was truly an incredible feat for the time, and those trips are well documented by remains left by the Phoenicians, the Phoenicians are also credited with a journey that still amazes people. According to Herodotus, the Egyptian king Nekau II (610-595 BC) commissioned a Phoenician expedition to sail around Libya–the word the Greeks used for all of Africa outside of Egypt. Apparently, the expedition began somewhere in the Nile Delta (probably the capital city of Memphis) and then travelled through man-made canals until it reached the Red Sea, where it began its long sea voyage. Herodotus wrote, "In view of what I have said, I cannot but be surprised at the method of mapping Libya, Asia, and Europe. The three continents do, in fact, differ very greatly in size. Europe is as long as the other two put together, and for breadth is not, in my opinion, even to be compared to them. As for Libya, we know that it is washed on all sides by the sea except where it joins Asia, as was first demonstrated, so far as

---

[89] Ball, 2010
[90] Bagnall, R. S. (2011) *The Oxford Handbook of Papyrology*. Oxford: Oxford University Press
[91] Schmitz, P. C. (2002) "Reconsidering a Phoenician Inscribed Amulet from the Vicinity of Tyre." *Journal of the American Oriental Society*, 122: 4. 817 - 823

our knowledge goes, by the Egyptian king Neco, who, after calling off the construction of the canal between the Nile and the Arabian gulf, sent out a fleet manned by a Phoenician crew with orders to sail round and return to Egypt and the Mediterranean by way of the Pillars of Heracles. The Phoenicians sailed from the Red Sea into the southern ocean, and every autumn put in where they were on the Libyan coast, sowed a patch of ground, and waited for next year's harvest. Then, having got in their grain, they put to sea again, and after two full years rounded the Pillars of Heracles in the course of the third, and returned to Egypt. These men made a statement which I do not myself believe, though others may, to the effect that as they sailed on a westerly course round the southern end of Libya, they had the sun on their right–to northward of them. This is how Libya was first discovered to be surrounded by sea, and the next people to make a similar report were the Carthaginians." (Herodotus, *Histories*, IV, 42-43).

This passage reveals some interesting points, particularly the fact that Herodotus does not believe the account without stating his reasons. Perhaps he found the crew's statement of the position of the sun confusing and unbelievable and therefore deduced that they lied, but the science supports the account. If they sailed around Africa starting in the Indian Ocean, then the sun would have been exactly where Herodotus stated it was. At this point, Herodotus' account cannot be corroborated by any other primary sources, but it is amazing to consider that a crew of Phoenicians may have been the first people to circumnavigate Africa, over 2,000 before Vasco de Gama did it for Portugal in the late 15th century.

**Chapter 2: Early Phoenician History**

**The Phoenician Entrepôt**

In the 2nd millennium BCE, there was a definite upheaval in Near Eastern society, including the fall of the Hittite Empire, the destruction of sites on Cyprus (including Enkomi), and the fall of powerful cities on the Levantine coast such as Ugarit.[92] In the resulting power vacuum, the major Phoenician cities emerged as independent city states and created their own flourishing maritime empire.

By approximately 1200 BCE, the Bronze Age town of Byblos had been destroyed, like many other cities along the Levantine coast, by the invasion of the Sea Peoples. The empires that had dominated the Levant for so long, including the Egyptians and Hittites, were severely weakened, and now that Byblos was free from Egyptian and Hittite dominance, the new residents could rebuild it as an independent city state. It soon became the major center of intellectual, commercial, and artistic activities, and Phoenician trade from the city dominated the Mediterranean Sea routes for the next 200 years.

Intellectual life was marked by the invention of the Phoenician alphabet in this time, and Byblos has yielded almost all of the known examples of inscriptions in the Phoenician alphabet, most of them dating to the 10th century BCE. These include the earliest examples of the Phoenician alphabet, 38 words etched onto the sarcophagus of King Ahiram, who died in approximately 1020 BCE.[93] Ahiram was buried in the Byblos necropolis, and like his predecessors he was interred within a sarcophagus. This bore a domed lid supported by four pouncing lions, and the walls of his tomb depicted long processions and winged sphinxes.[94] Evidence suggests that the walls were painted in rich colors.

The invention of the alphabet obviously facilitated the smooth operation of their maritime trade, and through it the Phoenicians spread the use of their alphabet to Lebanon, Syria, Israel, Cyprus, North Africa, and Europe. It was adopted by the Greeks, who later passed it to the Etruscans and Romans.[95] According to the 1st century CE Roman writer Pliny the Elder, "I am of the opinion that the Assyrians have always had writing, but others, such as Gellius, hold that it was invented in Egypt by Mercury, while others think it was discovered in Syria; both schools of thought believe that Cadmus imported an alphabet of 16 letters into Greece from Phoenicia..."[96].

---

[92] D'Amato R., and Salimbeti, A. (2015) *The Sea Peoples of the Mediterranean Bronze Age 1450–1100 BC*. London: Osprey
[93] Albright, W. F. (1947) "The Phoenician Inscriptions of the Tenth Century BC from Byblus." *Journal of the American Oriental Society*, 67(3). 153 - 160.
[94] Haran, M. (1958) "The Bas-Reliefs on the Sarcophagus of Ahiram King of Byblos in the Light of Archaeological and Literary Parallels from the Ancient Near East." *Israel Exploration Journal*, 8(1). 15 - 25.
[95] Mavrojannis, T. (2007) "Herodotus on the Introduction of the Phoenician Alphabet to the Greeks, the Gephyraeans and the Proto-Geometric Building at Toumba in Lefkandi." *Klio-Beiträge zur Alten Geschichte*, 89(2). 291 – 319
[96] Azevedo, J. (1994) "The origin and transmission of the alphabet." *Andrews University Digital Library of Dissertations and Theses*

King Ahiram was succeeded by his son, Ethbaal, who reigned until approximately 980 BCE, when he was succeeded by his son Yahimelek (950–940 BCE). The late 11th and early 10th centuries were a time of great upheaval in the region. King David (1010–970 BCE) created a united Jewish kingdom in the land of Israel, and around the same time the power of Byblos was surpassed by Tyre, then ruled by King Hiram I the Great (978–944), who had gained great wealth through an alliance with the Hebrew king Solomon in which Hiram provided cedar wood for the construction of Solomon's magnificent temple in Jerusalem. In the Bible, it was written that "Hiram king of Tyre sent messengers to David, and cedar trees, and carpenters and masons. And they built David a house."[97] Though the city continued to flourish well into the Roman period, Byblos never fully recovered its former supremacy in the region.

In the 8th century BCE, the Phoenicians found themselves threatened by a new great power in the north east: the Neo-Assyrian Empire. From their homeland in northern Mesopotamia, the Neo-Assyrians spread their political and cultural hegemony across the coastal Near East, and King Shipitsbaal of Byblos (750–738 BCE) was forced to become a vassal to the Neo-Assyrian emperor Tiglath Pileser III, in 738 BCE.[98] The next ruler, Sennacherib (705–681 BCE), completed the task, putting down rebellions at Tyre and taking over all of Phoenicia. In 701 BCE Sennacherib plundered Byblos, which was then ruled by King Ormelek I. Ormelek I's successor, King Melekiasaph, faced further attacks by the Assyrian kings Esarhaddon and Ashurbanipal.

---

[97] 2 Samuel, 5:11; see also 2 Chronicles, 2:11-14
[98] Oded, B. (1974) "The Phoenician cities and the Assyrian Empire in the time of Tiglath-pileser III." *Zeitschrift des Deutschen Palästina-Vereins*, 1. 38 - 49.

Tiglath Pileser III

**A depiction of Sennacherib on his palace in Nineveh**

After the fall of the Neo-Assyrian Empire in 609 BCE the Phoenician city-states were briefly dominated by the Babylonians, but Byblos changed hands again in 539 BCE with the invasion of the Achaemenid Persians under Cyrus the Great (559–529 BCE). Phoenicia was then divided into four vassal kingdoms: Sidon, Tyre, the island of Arwad, and Byblos. These cities served as the ports of the Persian fleets, and most of them flourished once more as they enjoyed the benefits of Persian rule.

The Bible and other Christian texts have served as key sources of information for this period of history. In the book of Ezekiel (622–570 BCE), Byblos was described as the biggest naval shipyard in ancient times, a role that continued well into the 1st millennium CE. The city contributed to the construction of Persian ships, and its fleet was drawn upon during the wars between Persia and Greece throughout the 5th century BCE.[99] Important architectural works were built throughout the city, especially focusing on the site's defenses and harbor, and the sanctuary of Ba'alat Gebal was restored.[100]

**Clash of Civilizations**

The rise of Hellenistic powers in the 4th century BCE gradually overcame the last vestiges of ancient Phoenicia. In November 333 BCE, Alexander the Great, king of Macedonia, defeated the last Persian emperor, Darius III, after which the famous conqueror continued to the Phoenician

---

[99] Wallinga, H. T. (2005) *Xerxes' Greek adventure: the naval perspective*. Brill.
[100] Sala, 2012

coast. The port-cities represented a threat to Alexander since they harbored the bulk of the Persian fleet and presented a key threat to the Aegean.[101] Many of the cities in the region surrendered to Alexander voluntarily and peacefully, apart from Tyre, where one of the most famous sieges of antiquity finally subdued the Phoenician stronghold and marked the end of the Phoenicians as a power in the region.[102] Byblos surrendered quietly, though the Temple of Resheph was destroyed during the time of Alexander the Great.[103]

**Andrew Dunn's picture of a bust of Alexander the Great**

---

[101] Bosworth, A. B. (1993) *Conquest and Empire: the reign of Alexander the Great*. Cambridge University Press.
[102] Bosworth, 1993
[103] Sala, 2012

**A picture of the ancient city's ramparts**

**A picture of the ruins of a Persian castle at Byblos**

Due to pressure from their neighbors, and their own internal discord, the Phoenicians and their former role in long-distance Mediterranean maritime trade gradually declined, but their colony at Carthage continued to prosper though the mining of iron and precious metals on the Iberian Peninsula, and through its considerable naval force and mercenary army. Carthage would remain a great power until it was finally destroyed by Rome in 146 BCE at the end of the Punic Wars.[104]

Liberated from the yoke of Persian rule, Byblos once again became a significant trade center oriented westwards towards the Aegean. Coins were minted there, and many parts of the city were rebuilt, including the temple areas.[105] During this time, Byblos also became the main center of worship of Adonis, the mortal lover of Aphrodite and a pervasive figure across the Mediterranean world. Adonis was the son of an incestuous relationship between Cinyrus, king of Cyprus, and his daughter Myrrha.[106] To escape from her father, who was enraged for being

---

[104] Charles-Picard, G., and Charles-Picard, C. (1968) *The life and death of Carthage: a survey of Punic history and culture from its birth to the final tragedy.* Pan Macmillan.
[105] Betlyon, J. W. (1982) *The coinage and mints of Phoenicia: the pre-Alexandrine period.* Scholars Press.
[106] Berner, U. (2008) "Mircea Eliade and the Myth of Adonis." *International Eliade*, 37

deceived into sleeping with her, Myrrha begged for assistance from the heavens. According to the Roman poet Ovid, an unknown goddess transformed Myrrha into a tree, thus rescuing her from Cinyrus and sparing her of punishment in the underworld for her wicked deeds.

9 months later, from the trunk of the tree Adonis was born. Aphrodite, the goddess of beauty and love, was nearby and was accidentally pierced by one of her son, Cupid's, arrows. She became besotted with Adonis. Persephone, the goddess of the underworld, also fell in love with the boy, and Adonis had to spend half of the year with each of the goddesses. One day, when Aphrodite was away and Adonis was hunting in the forest, he came upon a wild boar, an animal that she had warned him to avoid. The young hunter boldly attacked the beast, but the boar charged in retaliation and gorged upon the young man's thigh. As Adonis lay dying on the forest floor, his cries reached Aphrodite, and she rushed down to comfort him as he passed away.

Unwilling to let his memory pass into the mists of time, Aphrodite sprinkled his corpse with nectar, transforming him into a red flower, the Anemone. These events were supposed to have taken place near Byblos, the landscape of which is still filled with Anemone to this day.[107] For this reason, a festival commemorating the resurrection of Adonis has been held each spring when the Anemone bloomed, right up to the present day. Only women were involved in the ceremonies, which took place over two days, the first being devoted to mourning and the second to celebration. For ancient people the life of Adonis, shared between the living and the underworld, became a symbol of the vacillations between spring and winter, seasons of life and death.

After the death of Alexander the Great, the region was controlled by a succession of Hellenistic rulers: in 323 Laomedon of Mytilene, in 320 Ptolemy I Soter (King of Egypt from 305-282), in 315 Antigonus I Monophtalmos (King of Macedonia from 306-301), in 301 Demetrios I Poliorcetes (King of Macedonia from 294-287), and in 296 the Seleucid king, Seleucus I Nikator (305-280).[108] Between 286 and 197 BCE, the former lands of Phoenicia were under the control of Ptolemy of Egypt, although Tyre later became autonomous in 126 BCE, followed by Sidon in 111 BCE. Phoenicia was taken over by the Armenian king, Tigran (95–54 BCE) in approximately 82 BCE. After his loss to the Roman statesman and general Lucius Licinius Lucullus in 69 BCE, Phoenicia was incorporated into the Roman province of Syria.

---

[107] Dunand, 1973
[108] Jidéjian, 1968

**Engraving of a bust of Lucullus**

During the three centuries of Roman rule between 64 BCE and 330 CE, Byblos enjoyed the benefits of living under the Pax Romana. The Romans enriched the city with temples, baths and mosaics, and they built colonnaded streets within the urban center. They also connected the city to other towns as far away as Damascus with an extensive infrastructure across the region.[109]

---

[109] Saghieh, 1975

**A picture of the remains of a Roman colonnaded street**

In the 3rd century CE a small but impressive theater was built; there were originally 30 rows of stone benches, but much of the theatre was torn down and recycled by the city's later inhabitants.[110] Holes in the first tier of benches are believed to have been used to fix poles which would have enabled the seats to be covered by an awning during wet or sunny weather. A mosaic of Bacchus, the god of wine, was in the center of the theater, which also featured carved friezes, Corinthian columns, and an altar.[111]

---

[110] Retzleff, A. (2003) "Near Eastern theatres in late antiquity." *Phoenix*, 115 - 138.
[111] Jidéjian, 1968

**Remains of the Roman theater**

It was during this period that Philo of Byblos (64–141 CE) lived. A Phoenician-Roman scholar and client of the consul Herennius Severus, Philo wrote a great number of grammars, lexicons, encyclopedias, and historical texts about scientists and famous figures. His best known work is a translation of the history of the Phoenicians written up to two millennia earlier by a Phoenician resident of Byblos named Sanchuniathon.[112]

Sanchuniathon was a priest in Byblos who compiled a selection of oral histories into his text, one of the earliest to have been written in the region. It described an entire mythos: life before the Great Flood, with descriptions of the first mortals; the invention of fire, housing, and clothing; and the origins of art, agriculture, and navigation.[113] At the same time, there was enough historical grounding in the work that Philo's translation into Greek represents one of the best sources of information on ancient Phoenician society. Philo also provided evidence of the close connection between Egypt and Byblos in 2000 BCE; one of the writers that he writes of is Taautos of Byblos, known in Egypt as the ibis-headed god Thoth, who is credited with the invention of writing and the alphabet.[114]

---

[112] Baumgarten, A. I. (1981) *The Phoenician History of Philo of Byblos: A Commentary*. Brill.
[113] Baumgarten, 1981

The division of the Roman Empire in 395 CE under the reign of Emperor Theodosius I (r. 379–395 CE) resulted in Byblos being passed into the hands of the Byzantines, rulers of the Eastern Roman Empire. However, there has been very little evidence recovered from this time in the city other than traces of a mosaic and the foundations of a church close to the later site of the Cathedral of St. John the Baptist. Byblos was captured by the Arabs in 637 BCE, and it remained under their control until the arrival of the Crusaders.

A series of earthquakes hit the Lebanese coastline in the 6th century CE, causing widespread destruction in the old Phoenician cities. In 551 CE a particularly bad shockwave and tsunami destroyed the Phoenician city of Beirut, with an estimated 30,000 people dying in the disaster and many of the coastal cities reduced to ruins.[115]

In the resulting chaos, a new power swept across the Levant: the Arabs. The Sassanid king, Khusrau II, swept over the Near East from 613 CE, and by 637 CE most of the old cities of Phoenicia had been captured by the Sassanid general (and companion of the prophet Mohammad) Yazid ibn Abu Sufyan.[116] By 637 CE the Arabs were in total control of the region. Islam was then widely adopted in the major urban centers, and mosques were founded in Byblos.[117] Arabic became the *lingua franca* of administration. After a period of time Byblos once again began to revive, thanks in part to agricultural programs in its hinterland.

In 661 CE, Muawiyah I, the governor of Syria and founder of Umayyad Dynasty, was declared caliph, and Byblos became a key shipyard and harbor for the Umayyad fleet during their reign. During the 10th century Christian trade in the Mediterranean began to grow in size and influence, with the rise of the maritime powers of Venice, Amalfi, Pisa, and Genoa against the Arabs. Gradually, Italian Christian merchant guilds began to replace the old Phoenician trade and travel network of the Mediterranean.

In 969 CE the Umayyads were replaced by the Fatimid Dynasty based in Cairo, and later in the 11th century the Seljuk Turks emerged in Anatolia. These Muslim powers presented worrying threats to Byzantium and the Holy Roman Empire alike, and in 1095 CE Pope Urban II declared the First Crusade at the Council of Clermont, marking the beginning of three centuries of invasions in the Holy Land.[118] The effects of these campaigns continue to be felt politically throughout the modern Middle East, but during the Crusader period, the land of Phoenicia became divided between two Crusader kingdoms: the County of Tripoli to the north, and the Latin Kingdom of Jerusalem to the south. Byblos was incorporated into the County of Tripoli.

---

[114] Edwards, M. J. (1991) "Philo or Sanchuniathon? A Phoenicean Cosmogony." *The Classical Quarterly (New Series)*, *41*(01). 213 - 220.
[115] Darawcheh, R., Sbeinati, M. R., Margottini, C., and Paolini, S. (2000) "The 9 July 551 AD Beirut earthquake, eastern Mediterranean region." *Journal of Earthquake Engineering, 4(04).* 403 - 414
[116] Holland, T. (2012) *In the shadow of the sword: the battle for global empire and the end of the ancient world.* Hachette UK
[117] Jidéjian, 1968
[118] Venning, T. (2015) *A Chronology of the Crusades.* London: Routledge

In 1097 an enormous army of European knights made its way to the Holy Land, capturing Jerusalem in 1099 and establishing the Latin Kingdom of Jerusalem with Godfrey of Bouillon as its first king.[119] During their crossing of the Holy Land, the European armies passed near Byblos–known to them as Gibelet–but initially did not attack the city. This was due to a non-aggression agreement they signed with the governor of Tripoli, Fakhr al-Mulk ibn-Ammar. The ancient city only came under the control of the Europeans when Raymond de Saint-Gilles, count of Tolouse, conquered it in April 1104 CE, with the invaluable help of a Genoese fleet of 40 galleys.[120] Raymond rewarded the Genoese by granting them control of a third of Byblos. In June 1109 CE Bertrand de Saint-Gilles, son of Count Raymond, donated the remaining portions of the city to the Genoese, following their assistance in his victory during the Siege of Tripoli between 1102 and 1109 CE.

One of the admirals of the Genoese fleet, Ugo Embriaco, eventually took charge of the administration of the whole city, and over time the Embriaco family effectively presented themselves as the lords and hereditary rulers of Byblos.[121] They became one of the most important families in the County of Tripoli.

The medieval city of Gibelet was defended by an enclosing wall with projecting towers built by the Crusaders. There was also a large castle built by the crusaders, and since it was one of the earliest built in the Holy Land, certain techniques and designs were used there for the very first time before being taken to other crusader castles around the region.[122] The plan was quite simple; it consisted of a rectangular courtyard and keep, with formidable walls flanked by five towers of various sizes. A dungeon was accessed by a doorway set about 6 feet above the ground, which led into a vast vaulted room with a cistern in the middle. Persian monuments fitted into the structure indicate that earlier buildings were torn down and their materials recycled for its construction.[123] An elegant bridge with two arches served as the main entrance through the northern curtain wall.

---

[119] Venning, 2015
[120] Jidéjian, 1968
[121] Runciman, S. (1987) *A History of the Crusades*. Cambridge: Cambridge University Press.
[122] Kennedy, H. (2001) *Crusader castles*. Cambridge: Cambridge University Press.
[123] Jidéjian, 1968

**Pictures of the ruins of the Crusader castle**

**Artifacts in the museum inside the castle**

The second most spectacular building erected during the Crusades was the Cathedral of St. John the Baptist. With the rise of Christianity, Byblos had become a bishopric, and this structure was built over a number of stages throughout the 12th and 13th century.[124] Founded in 1115 CE, the original structure had three naves ending with a semi-circular apse, and an Italianate cupola and baptistery were later added in the northwestern side. A second church was also founded during this time, the Greek-Orthodox Saydet al-Najat Church (Church of Our Lady of Deliverance). The structure was built atop the ruins of an earlier Byzantine chapel, and many elements of the former building and others dating from the Roman period were reused in its construction.[125]

---

[124] Barton, J. M. (1933) "The Maronite Church of Syria." *Thought*, 7(4). 602 - 618.
[125] Jidéjian, 1968

**A picture of the cathedral**

In response to the Crusaders' initial victories, the sultan of the newly unified Ayyubid dynasty, Saladin, embarked on a number of campaigns across the Holy Land and eastern Mediterranean. Following his key victory at the Horns of Hattin in 1187, the crusader territories of the Holy Land gradually began to succumb to the Arab armies.[126] Ugo III Embriaco was captured at the Battle of Hattin, and Byblos was given to Saladin in August 1187 in exchange for the freedom of their lord. Fearing the arrival of Frederick Barbarossa, the Sultan ordered that many of the city's fortifications, including the crusader castle, be dismantled. However, a decade later the Embriaco family recovered their stronghold through the diplomatic skills of Stephanie of Milly, widow of the late Ugo III Embriaco (d. 1196). According to popular accounts, she managed to trick or bribe the Muslim guard of the city gates to open them and grant access to the Embriaco family's armies, who quickly overcame the defending forces.[127]

In the later stages of the 13th century, the Crusaders would have other problems. The invasion of the Mongol horde from the Central Eurasian steppe in 1243, the rise in power of the Muslim Mamelukes in Egypt, and later the sudden growth of the Ottoman Turks in Anatolia shifted the attention of the Crusaders away from the Holy Lands and towards preventing the spread of Islam

---

[126] Venning, 2015
[127] Jidéjian, 1968

into Europe.[128] With the County of Tripoli in shreds after the capture of its capital in 1289 by the Mameluke Sultan Qalawun, most of the Europeans in the region chose to evacuate. Nonetheless, Pietro Embriaco of Gibelletto seems to have convinced the Sultan to allow him to remain in Gibelet, on the condition of his close vassalage.[129] Pietro was the last recorded member of the Embriaco family to have ruled in Gibelet. When the Crusaders eventually left the Holy Land and retreated from their Near Eastern strongholds, Byblos generally declined into a small fishing village under the Mamelukes. That said, the Mamelukes did invest a certain amount of effort into rebuilding the Crusader-era fortifications in the site and built a mosque.[130]

**Byblos in the Modern Period**

The Ottoman Empire came from Anatolia in the 14th century and quickly spread across the Near East and North Africa following the defeat of the Mamelukes in the 16th century. Harbor installations, storage for merchants, mosques, and schools were built in the major cities of Lebanon, and the Ottomans took control of Byblos in 1516 following the Battle of Marj Dabik. The city then served as the capital of the Ottoman suburb of Jbeil, which incorporated more than 80 other villages and towns in its territory.[131] Semi-fortified warehouses, customs, and other commercial structures were built at its waterfront, and the harbor walls were rebuilt with recycled materials that had been recovered from earlier structures, including Roman columns.[132] A small port garrison was also constantly stationed there.

This was the bustling mercantile area in the city, but the administrative, political, and military core of Byblos was focused on the ancient citadel. The Mosque of the Sultan Abd el-Majiid was built in 1648 upon the site of the Mameluke period mosque, and later renovations were carried out by Emir Youssef Chehab in 1783. This mosque was composed of a semi-spherical cupola and an octagonal minaret. A number of elite residences were constructed within the walled Old Town, which continued to serve a defensive function throughout the period.[133] Further construction projects took place throughout the 17th, 18th and 19th centuries, resulting in the development of the *souk* (a dense market area) close to the ancient city gate. A second church, the Saydet al-Bouebeh (Church of the Lady of the Gate), was also built in the 18th century above the northern gate of the city wall.

---

[128] Venning, 2015
[129] Runciman, 1987
[130] Jidéjian, 1968
[131] Dunand, 1973
[132] Dunand, 1973
[133] In 1840 the British bombarded Byblos, causing extensive damage to the harbor and severely damaging the Cathedral of St. John the Baptist.

Wadih El-Banna's picture of Sultan Abdul Majid mosque at Byblos

**The old souk in Byblos**

 Emir Youssef also gave the Cathedral of St. John the Baptist to the Maronite Christian community.[134] Since the Ottoman period, the Maronites have played an increasingly significant role in the religion of Lebanon. The history of the Maronites is one of persecution and martyrdom by the Monophysites (those who believed that Jesus has a single divine nature, rather than being both human and divine) for the sake of independence and their beliefs.[135] They were originally a monastic sect that gathered around the "House of Maron" in approximately 452 on the Orontes River in Syria. After the Council of Chalcedon and request of Pope Leo in 451, those Christians who defended their faith became known as Maronites after a hermit priest, Saint Maron, who lived near Antioch and engaged in a mission of healing until his death around 410. His disciples continued his mission, and many of the pagan inhabitants of the Lebanon Mountains converted to the Christian faith. In the valleys of Lebanon the Maronite church began to grow, safe from the severe persecutions that were being carried out against their Syrian brethren in the 7th century.[136]

---

[134] Jidéjian, 1968
[135] Barton, 1933
[136] Barton, 1933

The first archaeological excavations at Byblos were undertaken by the French historian Ernest Renan in 1860, commissioned by Napoleon III, and in 1869 a chance discovery was made close to the citadel. A large stele, known today as the Yehawmilk, was revealed standing upright between two carved stone lions.[137] Upon its face were carved scenes reminiscent of Egyptian art, but with an inscribed text in the Phoenician script. It is one of the finest examples of Phoenician art from the 1st millennium BCE. It depicts a commonly used motif throughout the region from that time: the Egyptian winged sun disk, and underneath is a female figure sitting upon a throne–perhaps the Egyptian goddess Hathor–greeting another, standing person. The text was translated in 1874, revealing that the stele was dedicated to Ba'alat Gebal by the pre-Phoenician King Yehawmilk.[138]

Systematic excavations only began at Byblos in 1921, under the French archaeologist Pierre Montet, and the royal necropolis at Byblos was discovered by chance following a landslide caused by heavy rain in February 1922. Located in the western side of the site, the necropolis featured several tombs, the oldest of which dated to the 2nd millennium BCE. Each tomb was between 27-35 feet deep.[139]

In 1926, Maurice Dunand resumed the work of Montet, and the site was extensively excavated for over 60 years between 1921 and 1983, when excavations had to cease due to the escalation of the Lebanese Civil War (1975–1990) in the area. The outbreak of this series of conflicts in Lebanon interrupted all archaeological research at Byblos, and only limited excavations and research studies have been undertaken on the city since the end of the war. The more recent fighting between Hezbollah and Israel in 2006 also had a negative impact on the city's environmental and cultural heritage, most notably when the walls of its ancient harbor were covered by an oil slick after the Jiyeh Power Station was bombed by Israeli airforces.[140] A cleaning mission was quickly undertaken by UNESCO and the International Centre for the Study of the Preservation and Restoration of Cultural Property (ICCROM), which managed to prevent further damage to the reused granite Roman columns of the harbor walls, the foundations of the medieval towers at the entrance to the port, and a fish tank on the sea shore dating from the Hellenistic period.[141]

Unfortunately, the excavation methods used during the time by Montet and Dunand differed greatly from those employed in present-day excavations, and the quality of information received is therefore not always satisfactory. They dug layers of an arbitrary depth–usually 20 centimeters–rather than by context and feature. Combined with their less-than-rigorous forms of cataloging the artifacts recovered, this has made it difficult to precisely establish their

---

[137] Gubel, É. (2002) *Art phénicien: la sculpture de tradition phénicienne*. Réunion des musées nationaux.
[138] Gubel, 2002
[139] Jidéjian, 1968
[140] Tahan, L. G. (2015) "Lebanon: Cultural Heritage Threatened by the War in Lebanon in 2006." *Heritage at Risk*, 107.
[141] Zaven, T. (2010) *Emergency Safeguarding of the World Heritage Site of Byblos*. Beirut: UNESCO

stratigraphic relationship with one another, which has had an impact on the creation of a relative chronology for the various phases of activity at Byblos.[142]

In 1984 Byblos became listed as a UNESCO World Heritage Site, the foremost criteria being its ancient age and association with the history and spread of the Phoenician alphabet.

**Online Resources**

Other books about ancient history by Charles River Editors

Other books about the Phoenicians on Amazon

**Bibliography**

Arrian. 1971. *The Campaigns of Alexander.* Translated by Aubrey de Sélincourt. London: Penguin Books.

Bagnall, Nigel. 2002. *The Punic Wars: 246-146 BC.* London: Osprey Publishing.

Berlin, Andrea M. 1997. "From Monarchy to Markets: The Phoenicians in Hellenistic Palestine." *Bulletin of the American Schools of Oriental Research* 306: 75-88.

Bikai, Patricia Maynor. 1989. "Cyprus and the Phoenicians." *Biblical Archaeologist* 52: 203 209.

Breasted, James Henry, ed. and trans. 2001. *Ancient Records of Egypt.* Vol. 2, *The Eighteenth Dynasty.* Chicago: University of Illinois Press.

Cochavi-Rainey, Zipora, trans and ed. 1999. *Royal Gifts in the Late Bronze Age Fourteenth to Thirteenth Centuries B.C.E.: Selected Texts Recording Gifts to Royal Personages.* Jerusalem: Ben-Gurion University of the Negev Press.

Crawford, Michael. 2001. "Early Rome and Italy." In *The Oxford history of the Roman world,* ed. John Boardman, Jasper Griffin, and Oswyn Murray, 50-73. Oxford: Oxford University Press.

Diodorus. 2004. *The Library of History.* Translated by C.H. Oldfather. Cambridge, Massachusetts: Harvard University Press.

Herm, Gerhard. 1975. *The Phoenicians: The Purple Empire of the Ancient Near East.* Translated by Caroline Hillier. New York: William Morrow and Company.

---

[142] Breen, C., Forsythe, W., O'Connor, M., and Westley, K. (2014) *The Mamluk/Ottoman-period Maritime Cultural Landscape of Lebanon.* Coleraine: University of Ulster Centre for Maritime Archaeology

Herodotus. 2003. *The Histories*. Translated by Aubrey de Sélincourt. London: Penguin Books.

Kuhrt, Amélie. 2010. *The Ancient Near East: c. 3000-330 BC*. 2 vols. London: Routledge.

Lichtheim, Miriam, ed. 1976. *Ancient Egyptian Literature*. Vol. 2, *The New Kingdom*. Los Angeles: University of California Press.

Livy. 1996. *The War with Hannibal*. Translated by Aubrey de Sélincourt. London: Penguin Books.

Lloyd, Alan B. 1975. "Were Necho's Triremes Phoenician?" *Journal of Hellenic Studies* 95: 45- 61.

Lucas, A. and J.R. Harris. 1999. *Ancient Egyptian Materials and Industries*. Mineola, New York: Dover Publications.

Luckenbill, Daniel David, trans. and ed. 1989. *Ancient Records of Assyria and Babylonia*. 2 vols. London: Histories and Mysteries of Man.

Markoe, Glenn E. 2000. *Phoenicians*. Los Angeles: University of California Press.

Moran, William L. ed. and trans. 1992. *The Amarna Letters*. Baltimore: John Hopkins University Press.

Morkot, Robert. 1996. *The Penguin Historical Atlas of Ancient Greece*. London: Penguin Books.

Moscati, Sabatino. 1968. *The World of the Phoenicians*. Translated by Alastair Hamilton. New York: Frederick A. Praeger.

Noureddine, Ibrahim. 2010. "New Light on the Phoenician Harbor at Tyre." *Near Eastern Archaeology* 73: 176-181.

Pritchard, James B, ed. 1992. *Ancient Near Eastern Texts Relating to the Old Testament*. 3rd ed. Princeton, New Jersey: Princeton University Press.

Scarre, Chris. 1995. *The Penguin Historical Atlas of Ancient Rome*. London: Penguin Books.

Stern, E. 1990. "New Evidence from Dor for the First Appearance of the Phoenicians along the Northern Coast of Israel." *Bulletin of the American Schools of Oriental Research* 279: 27-34.

Strabo. 2001. *Geography*. Translated by Horace Leonard Jones. Cambridge, Massachusetts: Harvard University Press.

Watson-Treumann, Brigette. 2001. "Beyond the Cedars of Lebanon: Phoenician Timber Merchants and Trees from the 'Black Mountain.'" *Die Welt des Orients* 31: 75-83.

Wright, Edmund, ed. 2006. *A Dictionary of World History*. 2$^{nd}$ ed. Oxford: Oxford University Press.

Xenophon. 1972. *The Persian Expedition*. Translated by Rex Warner. London: Penguin Books.

## Free Books by Charles River Editors

We have brand new titles available for free most days of the week. To see which of our titles are currently free, click on this link.

## Discounted Books by Charles River Editors

We have titles at a discount price of just 99 cents everyday. To see which of our titles are currently 99 cents, click on this link.

Made in the USA
Middletown, DE
11 March 2023